THERE ONCE WAS A MAN WITH SIX WIVES

A Right Royal History in Limericks

Mick Twister

PORTICO

INTRODUCTION

THIS BOOK CONTAINS NUMEROUS RHYMES ON RULERS OF EARLIER TIMES, WITH BRIEF MNEMONICS DISTINGUISHING MONARCHS, THEIR LIVES, LOVES, ACHIEVEMENTS AND CRIMES.

This is a history of the kings and queens who ruled in England/Great Britain from Alfred the Great onwards. You could make a case for the earlier Offa or the later Edgar as the first English king, but you have to start somewhere.

I've included some Scots, Welsh, and Irish royals from the periods when those nations had rulers in their own right, and a few European rulers, who get in either because they made a significant mark or because they were colourful, interesting or floridly insane, and make for a good limerick.

Why write a limerick history of kings and queens? Well, as I said in the introduction to my previous book *There Was an Old Geezer Called Caesar*, the form is more suited to telling history through characters than broad themes.

Here are some observations that have struck me along the way:

 A lot of English kings and queens weren't all that English. The country's been ruled by native speakers of Danish, Norman, French, Dutch and German.

 Wars between nations were often family squabbles within an interconnected Euro-royalty over which sibling inherited which crown.

 Although your parent being a monarch is the best determining factor for becoming one yourself, there were an awful lot of points where the succession was unclear.

 Categorisation of the good, the bad and the ugly among monarchs, and tales of their noble or dastardly deeds, was often spun for political purposes.

Some of that is explored in the fact boxes. Along with the verses, I hope they will help readers to remember things about this or that monarch. You never know when they'll come in useful – in an exam, a pub quiz or a heated debate about a costume drama, perhaps.

ALFRED THE GREAT

THE CAKE-BURNER ALFRED THE GREAT,
CRAP BAKER, NOT BAD HEAD OF STATE,
TOOK RATHER A LIKING
TO GUTHRUM THE VIKING,
HIS FOE TURNING INTO HIS MATE.

The main story everyone learns about Alfred the Great is how, when times were hard, he hid in a swineherd's cottage, and the mistress of the house had a go at him for letting her cakes burn. It's meant to show that his mind was on higher things – but perhaps he was just used to having someone else to keep an eye on domestic matters for him.

His father was King of Wessex, but Alf had greater ambitions. He built a fleet of proper ships, and pushed the Vikings back to just the north and the east of England – i.e. about half of it. Magnanimous in victory, he made his Viking opponent Guthrum an offer he couldn't refuse – I won't kill you if you convert to Christianity and let me be your godfather. History records that thereafter they were firm friends, but maybe the Viking just didn't want to die at the hands of the original Godfather.

Alfred the Great

Ruled Wessex and Mercia, 871–899.   **King because** His dad was.
Age at accession 22.   **Language** Anglo-Saxon.
Achievements Losing finalist, *Great British Bake Off*, 878.

KENNETH McALPINE

THE FIRST SCOTTISH KING, TO BE STRICT
WAS PROBABLY MORE OF A PICT
OR MAYBE A GAEL —
THERE'S MANY A TALE
AND OFTEN THEY ALL CONTRADICT.

Several decades before Alfred cornered enough of the southern bit of Britain to be considered King of England, a chap named Kenneth McAlpine had done something similar in Scotland. But what was Scotland, and who were the Scots?

Kenneth came from a line of Pictish kings, who ran what is now northern and eastern Scotland. The western part was ruled by the Gaels (although the Picts were a bit Gaelicised anyway). They later joined forces as the Kingdom of Alba – which is the Gaelic for Scotland but used in English to distinguish it from Scotland. Not to be confused with Albion, which means Britain, home of the Britons, found mainly in England and southern Scotland.

Anyway, never mind all that, Kenneth McAlpine was the First King of Scotland. Not to be confused with Idi Amin, the former Ugandan President, who called himself the Last King of Scotland.

Kenneth McAlpine

Ruled Scotland, 843–858 (roughly).
King because He defeated rivals.
Born Iona.   **First language** Gaelic.

EDWARD THE ELDER

THE SECRET OF EDWARD'S INCURSIONS (ACCORDING TO VARIOUS VERSIONS) IN MAKING HIS GAINS FROM NEIGHBOURING DANES WAS ETHELFLED, LADY OF MERCIANS.

Alfred's son Edward the Elder only got that nickname a century later to distinguish him from the next Edward.

The real elder was his big sister Ethelfled, who ran Mercia (the Midlands) while he ran Wessex.

Together they kicked the Danes out of East Anglia. Then when Ethel died in 918, Ed's control of England went all the way up to the Humber. Beyond that, the Northumbrian Vikings still ruled the roost.

Edward the Elder

Ruled Southern and central England, 899–924.
King because His dad Alfred was.
Base Winchester. **Achievements** Building forts.

ELFWEARD

YOUNG ELFWEARD WAS JUST ON THE THRONE
A FORTNIGHT, AS FAR AS IS KNOWN.
WHEN ASKED HOW HE DIED,
HIS BROTHER REPLIED,
'THE POOR KID WAS ACCIDENT-PRONE.'

Poor old Elfweard. A bookish type, he'd been living as a hermit when his old man Edward died, and he got called in to be king. Or maybe he didn't. No one is quite sure whether he ever got as far as perching his posterior on the throne of Wessex, never mind Mercia or East Anglia.

It may not have been an allergy as such, but something about being king didn't agree with him. That something may well have been his brother Athelstan, who succeeded him. If so, he managed to cover his traces well and make Elfweard's death look natural (not weird).

Elfweard
Ruled (kind of) Wessex, 16 July–1 August 924.
King because His dad Edward was.   **Cause of death** Allergy to crowns?
Achievements Managed to cross 'become king' off bucket list before he died.

ATHELSTAN

KING ATHELSTAN, SO IT IS WRITTEN,
TOOK OVER A GREAT DEAL OF BRITAIN;
HIS ARMY WENT FORTH
TO CONQUER THE NORTH
WHERE CONSTANTINE'S FORCES WERE SMITTEN.

Athelstan's coronation at Kingston upon Thames was the first with an actual crown, rather than a helmet. But the helmet still came in useful. He spent a lot of his energy on warfare, invading the north of England and even Scotland, while insisting the Welsh kings paid tribute and recognised him as boss.

He was also keen on law and order, and worried about the rising crime rate, especially robberies. He brought in the death penalty for anyone over 12 stealing anything worth more than eight pence. But then he admitted this harsh policy wasn't working – and kindly raised the minimum age to 15.

Athelstan

Ruled England, 924–939.
King because His dad Edward was.   **Age at accession** 30.
Achievements Tough on juvenile offenders.

EDMUND I

KING EDMUND THE FIRST'S TIME AS CHIEF
WAS BRUTALLY RENDERED QUITE BRIEF;
KING ED LOST HIS LIFE
WHEN STABBED WITH A KNIFE
BY SOMEONE HE'D NAMED AS A THIEF.

King Edmund is buried at Glastonbury, renowned nowadays for its
peace-loving festival. But he came a cropper when security guards
at a feast in nearby Pucklechurch failed to deal with a man Edmund
recognised as a thief, whom he had previously exiled. Well, that's one
story. Others have suggested Edmund may have been assassinated by
enemies. Or someone trying to get his 'Access all areas' pass.

   During his six-year reign he lost the north of England, East Anglia
and the East Midlands to the Norse King Olaf of Dublin. Then when
Olaf died, Edmund attacked his son (also called Olaf) and won it back
again. Who knows how long this to-ing and fro-ing could have gone on
if only he hadn't been stabbed!

Edmund I

Ruled England, 939–946.
King because His dad Edward was.   **Age at accession** 18.
Achievements Lost the North then got it back again.

EDRED

KING EDRED HAD PROBLEMS WITH FOOD
WHICH SOME PEOPLE FOUND A BIT RUDE;
HE'D SUCK OUT THE JUICE
HIS FOOD WOULD PRODUCE
THEN SPIT OUT THE BITS HE HAD CHEWED.

Edred continued Edmund's back-and-forth battles with the Vikings of York. They kept winding him up by naming Erik Bloodaxe their king when he told them not to. If you want to know whether Erik preferred fighting or talking, the clue's in the name. Mind you, Edred himself wasn't averse to burning down the odd monastery (Ripon, to be precise) to teach those uppity Northerners a lesson.

It's a shame Edred's mainly remembered for his table manners, which seem to have been caused by a digestive problem that meant he could only digest liquids. Nowadays he'd just have bought a juicer and lived on smoothies.

Edred

Ruled England, 946–955.
King because His dad Edward was. **Cause of death** Gut trouble.
Achievements Ended Viking rule in northern England.

BRIAN BORU

THE IRISH KING BRIAN BORU
TOOK POWER BY MEANS OF A COUP,
UNITING THE ISLE,
IF JUST FOR A WHILE,
AS NORDIC INVADERS WITHDREW.

Although Brian Boru is the best-remembered of the Irish kings, he was not born to the job. Ireland had been divided into many kingdoms, with a High King traditionally drawn from the O'Neill family.

But after winning a series of battles against the Vikings and other local rulers, Brian was able to persuade the O'Neill incumbent, Malachy II, to acknowledge him as High King. Briefly Brian had titular authority over more or less the whole island.

He died on Good Friday 1014 in the Battle of Clontarf, during which his united Irish forces routed the Viking army. The Viking fleet withdrew, but the Norse remained in Ireland, where they had already founded settlements including Dublin, Waterford, Cork and – of course – Limerick.

Brian Boru

Ruled Ireland, 1002–1014.
King because He fought his way to the top. **First language** Gaelic.
Legacy Everyone called O'Brien.

EDWIG

THE TEENAGE KING EDWIG, IT'S SAID,
RAN OFF WITH THE GIRL HE WOULD WED.
WHEN DUE TO BE CROWNED,
THE YOUNG MAN WAS FOUND
WITH HER AND HER MOTHER IN BED.

Edwig may sound like what a Cockney would call Harry Potter's owl, but he seems to have behaved rather unwisely. The first thing he did was to fall out with Dunstan, his father's favourite bishop and a powerful man.

So the story goes, he failed to turn up to a meeting with some of the nobles on his coronation day, and was discovered cavorting with his fiancée – and her mother. 'Mum's the Word – Randy Ed's Secret Three-in-a-bed Romps', as the *News of Ye World* reported it.

Dunstan dragged him off, calling the new king's wife-to-be a 'strumpet'. Edwig got his revenge, kicking the bishop out of the country, but his problems didn't end there. The pro-Dunstan thanes in the North switched allegiance to his brother Edgar, leaving him with only Wessex and Kent to rule.

Edwig

Ruled England, 955–959.
King because His dad Edmund was.
Age at accession 16.   **Cause of death** Mysterious illness.

EDGAR

KING EDGAR'S SUBLIME CORONATION WAS AIMED AT UNITING THE NATION, WITH GLORIOUS UNCTION PERFORMED AT A FUNCTION ANOINTING THE KING'S ORDINATION.

King Edgar was crowned in a bath of oil. No, hang on – he was crowned in Bath with oil. It was the first proper, recorded coronation. The use of oil was intended to echo the anointment of Solomon in the Old Testament. Edgar ruled England, but also received pledges of allegiance from the kings of almost all of Britain.

The first thing Edgar did as king was to bring Bishop Dunstan back from exile. This ensured that he would be remembered as Edgar the Peaceful, a wise, just ruler, when the priests came to write history. They glossed over minor indiscretions of his, such as killing a love rival and abducting his mistress from a nunnery.

Edgar

Ruled England, 959–975.
King because His dad Edmund was. **Age at accession** 15.
Achievements Getting rid of wolves.

EDWARD THE MARTYR

WHEN EDWARD WAS ONLY FIFTEEN,
HE STAYED WITH HIS STEPMUM, THE QUEEN,
WHO MADE HIM A MARTYR —
WHICH, HAD HE BEEN SMARTER,
THE YOUNG MONARCH MIGHT HAVE FORESEEN.

When Edgar died there was a power struggle between the sons of his different wives, complicated by disagreements over Dunstan's reform of the monasteries. Twelve-year-old Edward got there first, with the backing of Dunstan, but his kid brother Ethelred's mum Elfrida had it in for him.

Young Edward was only 15 and already three years on the throne when his stepmother invited him to come hunting at Corfe Castle in Dorset. Sadly, Ed failed to grasp that he was the quarry, and was stabbed by either Elfrida's or Ethelred's men as soon as he arrived.

Although he wasn't canonised, Edward was subsequently considered a martyr, and is still revered in the Russian Orthodox Church.

Edward the Martyr

Ruled England, 975–978. **King because** His dad Edgar was.
Achievements The odd miracle, allegedly. Big in Russia.
Cause of death Stabbing.

ETHELRED THE UNREADY

KING ETHELRED'S ENEMIES SAID HE
WAS BADLY ADVISED, NOT UNREADY.
A KING WITH MORE BRAINS
WOULD NOT SLAUGHTER DANES,
THUS MAKING HIS TENURE UNSTEADY.

'Unready' might seem a fairly obvious description for anyone taking over a country at the age of ten, but in fact it means 'bad advice' – a joke on the inappropriateness of the name Ethelred, which means 'good advice'. Whether it was just bad luck or a perception of weakness, Ethelred's reign saw the return of attacks by Danish ships along the east coast, and Ethelred's chosen solution was to buy them off by paying a tribute, known as the Danegeld.

When that didn't work, he had the bright idea, in 1002, of ordering the massacre of all Danes in England. It's not known how many were killed, but of course it didn't make their relatives over the water any friendlier.

Defeated by Sven Forkbeard, he fled to Normandy, where his wife Emma came from. But he outlived Sven and got another couple of years on the throne – apparently unready to retire.

Ethelred the Unready

Ruled England, 978–1016 (with a gap in 1013–14).
King because His dad Edgar was.   **Age at accession** 10.
Achievements Marrying a Norman.

SVEN FORKBEARD

THERE WAS AN OLD MAN WITH A BEARD
WHO SAID, 'IT IS JUST AS I FEARED;
THOUGH FOLKS ARE POLITE,
BECAUSE OF MY MIGHT
THEY ALL THINK MY FACE-HAIR IS WEIRD.'

Sven Forkbeard was so called because of the cleft in his beard. Which makes you wonder what they called him as a baby, and also how his father Harald Bluetooth got his name (did he have mysterious powers to communicate with people within a 100-metre range?).

From the beginning of the 11th century Sven launched repeated attacks on England, seeking bloody revenge for Ethelred's St Brice's Day massacre of Danes. Eventually in 2013 his fleet landed in Gainsborough, Lincolnshire, which must have had the element of surprise as it was 90km from the sea.

He was crowned King of England on Christmas Day 1013, but like a cheap Christmas present, or a New Year resolution, it was all over by early February. Sven's death is a mystery, but he had certainly made a lot of enemies. Or perhaps he was set upon by pogonophobes outraged by his hipster beard.

Sven Forkbeard

Ruled England, 25 December 1013–3 February 1014; Denmark/Norway, 986–1014.
King because He beat Ethelred.   **First language** Danish.
Legacy Services to facial hair.

EDMUND IRONSIDE

THERE ONCE WERE TWO RIVAL KINGS WHO
AGREED TO SPLIT ENGLAND IN TWO;
THIS WASN'T FULFILLED,
AS EDMUND GOT KILLED
ONE NIGHT AS HE SAT ON THE LOO.

Phew, back to kings called Ed-something, that's a relief!

Edmund Ironside's nickname came from his reputation for being tough in battle, mainly against the Danish King Canute, whom many bishops and other senior figures wanted instead of him. Edmund's forces defeated Canute's several times, which was a surprise as Denmark was a lot higher up in the Top Trumps world battle rankings in those days.

Looking for a route to getting back on top, Canute decided the only way was Essex, and the two sides met near Southend. Canute won, but the two kings agreed to partition the country between north and south. Alas, Edmund died a few weeks later in mysterious circumstances. One account has it that he was stabbed by someone hiding in the pit of the latrine where poor Edmund went to do his business.

Edmund Ironside

Ruled Southern England, April–November 1016.
King because His dad Ethelred was.
Age at accession 28.   **Cause of death** Toilet trouble.

CANUTE

THERE WAS AN OLD KING NAMED CANUTE
WHO CAME WITH A FEARSOME REPUTE,
BUT SHOWED HIS DECREE
STOPPED SHORT OF THE SEA —
HIS POWER WAS NOT ABSOLUTE.

King Canute, or Cnut the Great as he is known in Denmark, actually ruled England for longer than he did his homeland. The Anglo-Saxon chroniclers changed his name to Canute to make it sound more English (and possibly to avoid embarrassing typos).

His Viking conquest of England came amid an age of Scandinavian domination not seen again in Britain for almost a thousand years — until BBC4 started showing *Borgen* and *The Bridge* on Saturday nights.

He was known as a wise king, particularly for one incident, in which he went down to the sea near Southampton and commanded the waves to stay back. They didn't, of course, and his feet got wet. This a) proved to flattering courtiers that there were limits to his power, b) got him off the hook the next time the Somerset levels flooded, as flood defence was clearly outside his remit, and c) gave his smelly feet a much-needed wash.

Canute

Ruled England, 1016–1035; Denmark, 1018–1035; Norway/part of Sweden, 1028–1035. **King because** Conquest/death of Edmund Ironside.
Big adventure A pilgrimage to Rome, in the days before budget airlines.

HAROLD I

KING HAROLD DISLIKED HIS HALF-BROTHER,
THEY NEVER GOT ON WITH EACH OTHER;
SO WHEN CANUTE PASSED
HAREFOOT NIPPED IN FAST
AND EXILED POOR HARTHACNUT'S MOTHER.

Harold Harefoot did not get his name from his hairy feet – that would
have made him Hairfoot, obviously – but because he could run fast.
Nowadays, when politicians run for office you don't take it literally.
But back then you had to move quickly to get your hands on power.

Harthacnut was meant to succeed Canute as Danish and English king,
but he had his hands full in Denmark fighting off the Norwegians.
So his older half-brother Harold offered to keep the seat warm for him as
a regent. But Harthacnut took so long to get round to coming to claim
his throne that the nobles agreed Harold might as well be king anyway.
Harthacnut's mother, Emma of Normandy, fled to Bruges.

Accounts of Harold's death report that he was 'elf-shot' – which
is how the Anglo-Saxons described death from a mysterious,
unexplained illness.

Harold I

Ruled England, 1035–1040 (crowned 1037).
King because His dad Canute was.   **First language** Danish.
Cause of death Shot by elves?

HARTHACNUT

KING HARTHACNUT'S SIMPLE BIOG
GOES: 'DUMPED BROTHER'S BODY IN BOG;
RULED FOR TWO YEARS;
LIKED A FEW BEERS;
DIED OF A SURFEIT OF GROG.'

Harthacnut, aka Hardicnut, eventually made it to England once his mum was there to help him cross the Channel – only to find Harold Harefoot had died before he could kill him.

Blaming Harold for the death of his brother Alfred Etheling, Harthacnut had Harefoot's body dug up from its resting place in Westminster and reburied in a marsh or a sewer, according to various accounts.

But Harthacnut only had a few years to get stuck into the normal kingly things like raising taxes and burning down the villages of anyone who protested. He'd just stood up to toast the bride at the wedding of his friends Tovi and Gytha, when he suddenly collapsed and died, goblet in hand.

Harthacnut

Ruled Denmark, 1035–1042; England, 1040–1042.
King because His dad Canute was. **First language** Danish.
Cause of death Drink.

EDWARD THE CONFESSOR

**KING EDWARD WAS CALLED THE CONFESSOR,
A PIOUS OLD CHAP — SIMPLE DRESSER.
HE BUILT A BIG ABBEY,
HEALED FOLKS WHO WERE SCABBY,
BUT MESSED UP HIS CHOICE OF SUCCESSOR.**

Ethelred's son Edward was a deeply religious man. He didn't actually build Westminster Abbey himself, but 'commissioned the construction of' doesn't scan very well, so call it poetic licence. He was the first king supposed to have the royal touch, allowing him to heal a number of conditions including scrofula, also called 'the king's evil'.

The confessions of Edward the Confessor would have been pretty boring for the poor priest — Ed was celibate.

His limited sex life may have given Edward an insight into difficult marriages, but it also meant he had no children, which left the matter of succession up in the heir, as it were. He appears to have rashly promised the throne separately to William of Normandy and to his mate Earl Godwin's boy Harold. So he must have lied to one of them — I wonder whether he confessed that?

Edward the Confessor

Ruled England, 1042–1066.
King because His dad Ethelred was. **First language** English.
Legacy Patron saint of difficult marriages.

MACBETH

THOUGH SCOTLAND'S CROWN WENT TO MACBETH
ONCE DUNCAN EXHALED HIS LAST BREATH,
NO WIZENED OLD CRONES
IN THIS GAME OF THRONES
PREDICTED THE FORMER KING'S DEATH.

Most people who know anything about Macbeth know William
Shakespeare's version – met some witches who told him he would be
king, killed Duncan to make it happen, egged on by Lady Macbeth but
plagued by doubt and ghosts, killed by Macduff, Malcolm takes over.
But most accounts seem to agree Duncan was killed in battle – by
Macbeth's forces, but with no known supernatural involvement.

We don't know much about the real Macbeth. He fought the English
– something you had to get on your CV at some point as a Scottish king.
The real Lady Macbeth was a princess named Gruoch, who married him
after he killed her husband (his cousin).

Most intriguingly, Macbeth went to Rome on a pilgrimage for six
months in 1050. The ability to take a gap year like that suggests his
reign wasn't quite as brief and precarious as Shakespeare made out.

Macbeth

Ruled Scotland, 1040–1057.
King because He beat Duncan in battle.
First language Scots. **Career highlight** Tour of Rome in 1050.

HAROLD II

WHEN FOLKS SAW A LIGHT IN THE SKY
THEY RECKONED THE END MUST BE NIGH;
BUT DEATH MERELY BECKONED
FOR HAROLD THE SECOND
FOR WHOM IT WAS ONE IN THE EYE.

Harold Godwinson had the unusual honour of being chosen as king – by the main Saxon nobles who made up the Witan, a kind of aristocratic parliament. But not everyone was convinced. When what we now know to have been Halley's Comet then appeared, everyone took it as an omen. For Harold, perhaps it was.

He fought off one challenger, the confusingly named Harald Hardrada, at Stamford Bridge in Yorkshire. But then he had to rush back down to Hastings, Sussex, to take on William of Normandy. William reckoned not only had Edward the Confessor promised *him* the throne, but Harold had agreed to back his claim, during a booze cruise to Normandy a few years earlier.

Harold was killed at Hastings – according to some accounts, by an arrow in the eye. It was not the last time England would blame fixture congestion for a damaging defeat.

Harold II

Ruled England, 5 January– 14 October 1066.
King because Chosen by the Witan.   **Cause of death** In battle.
Legacy Centuries of Norman domination.

WILLIAM I

IN 1066, DATE OF DATES,
HISTORICAL RECORD RELATES,
THE ENGLISH WERE MASTERED
BY WILLIAM THE BASTARD
WHO GAVE ALL THEIR LAND TO HIS MATES.

William the Conqueror had to conquer somewhere, if only to get rid of the 'bastard' tag he was given because of his illegitimate birth. After conquering England, he religiously recorded residents, commissioned crenellated castles and ruthlessly repressed rebellions – especially in northern England. He could still be a bit of a bastard, to be honest.

Under him, Norman rule was entrenched, with most of the power, land and money in the hands of noblemen from across the water, while the Saxons were excluded – Saxon nobles had their property confiscated, while the ordinary people increasingly became serfs, tied to cultivating land for the new Norman overlords.

But though we now remember him as King of England, he spent most of his time in France, where he died and was buried. England was just an add-on.

William I

Ruled Normandy, 1035–1087; England, 1066–1087.
King because Conquest.   **First language** Norman French.
Legacy The Domesday Book – a kind of national tax return.

WILLIAM II

YOUNG WILLIAM WAS OPENLY GAY —
UNUSUAL BACK IN THE DAY.
ALLEGEDLY RUFUS
WAS SHOT BY A DOOFUS
WHOSE ARROW WENT SLIGHTLY ASTRAY.

William the Conqueror had three sons. He left Normandy to Robert, the eldest, and England to William, while Henry got some pocket money. What could be fairer? But you know how petty siblings can get about such things.

William Rufus, so called because of his ruddy complexion, got a bad press in the subsequent histories. That may have been because he was hostile to the church, and it was the churchmen who wrote the histories. It could also be homophobia – one monk wrote that Rufus surrounded himself with 'sodomites and fornicators', and he was condemned for growing his hair long and paying attention to fashion.

William fought with Robert over their respective territories, but it was Henry, the youngest, who had the last laugh – he was out hunting with William in the forest when one of their friends 'accidentally' shot the king with an arrow.

William II

Ruled England, 1087–1100. **King because** His dad William was.
First language Norman French.
Cause of death Assassination/poor marksmanship.

HENRY I

THE FATHER OF MANY A KID,
OLD HENRY THE FIRST OVERDID
HIS FAVOURITE DISH
OF WEIRD SUCKY FISH
(HE SHOULD HAVE JUST ORDERED THE SQUID).

Perhaps it was to distance himself from his gay brother, but Henry went all out to prove his heterosexuality by fathering as many children as he could. He had four with his English wife Ethel (who had to be called Matilda because Normans thought it sounded better) and about two dozen with assorted mistresses.

When not busy procreating, he found time to invade France, defeating his brother Robert and reuniting the two territories – but this time, Normandy was ruled from England (albeit by Normans).

Henry's cause of death, a surfeit of lampreys, is right up there in the annals of weird royal deaths. The lamprey is a primitive parasitic fishlike vertebrate that clamps its suckers onto its prey. Strangely, this delicacy has fallen out of fashion.

Henry I

Ruled England, 1100–1135; Normandy, 1106–1135.
King because His dad William was.   **First language** Norman French.
Cause of death A surfeit of lampreys.

MATILDA

THE EMPRESS MATILDA, OR MAUD,
WHO'D SERVED AS A RULER ABROAD,
HAD NO CORONATION
AS DISCRIMINATION
HAD NOT AT THAT TIME BEEN OUTLAWED.

Matilda, daughter of Henry I and mother of Henry II, was married off as a child to the Holy Roman Emperor, Henry V. So she spent her teens and twenties bossing Germany and Italy around as Empress Maud.

She'd finished there and moved on to husband number two when the vacancy for ruler of England/Normandy came up. Matilda must have felt pretty confident that she had some solid experience to back up her claim as the dead king's only surviving legitimate child. But the idea of a woman ruler caused many Anglo-Norman noblemen to splutter indignantly into their goblets of wine, so they were only too ready to back her rival Stephen instead.

When she finally beat him, she still couldn't get enough support from the (male) power-brokers to hold a coronation, so she tends to be left off the official roll of rulers.

Matilda

Ruled Germany and Italy, 1114–1125; England, 1141–1148 (disputed); Normandy, 1148–1167. **Queen (or not) because** Her father Henry was. **Age at accession** 11 (Holy Roman Empire); 39 (England).

STEPHEN

THERE WAS A FRENCH NOBLE NAMED STEPHEN
WHOSE RECORD AT BEST WAS UNEVEN;
ERRATIC AND PANICKY
NATIONWIDE ANARCHY
STEPHEN'S BEST KNOWN FOR ACHIEVIN'.

Having acceded to the throne by virtue of not being a woman, Stephen of Blois did his best to disprove any lazy myths and assumptions about men being natural rulers, good at fighting, having leadership qualities etc., by being really, really bad at everything.

As Stephen and Matilda fought for the throne, England descended into chaos, with rival barons raiding each other's villages. Matters were further confused by Stephen's wife being called Matilda, and his brother being called Henry – who switched to support the other Matilda at one point!

While Matilda (not Stephen's wife) and her husband Geoffrey took Normandy, England's other territories in France were seized by rival French nobles. Eventually, Stephen and Matilda reached a power-sharing agreement of sorts, under which he could stay in power, as long as he was succeeded by Henry (her son, not her father, dead ex-husband or Stephen's brother).

Stephen

Ruled England, 1135–1154. **King because** His grandad William I was.
First language French.
Achievements Hmm, can I get back to you on that one…?

BARELY REGAL
THE SHORTEST REIGNS

9 days

JANE GREY

Not enough time to get
a coronation robe made
to measure.

15 days

ELFWEARD

He was king, if at all, from
16 July to 1 August 924. At
least the days were long.

40 days

SVEN FORKBEARD

Sven got a proper
crown for Christmas
1013, not a paper
one. Alas, he
lost it on
3 February.

3 months

EDWARD V

12-year-old Edward
lasted a quarter
of a year under
Uncle Richard's
protection, before
being deposed and
disappearing.

7 months

EDMUND IRONSIDE

April to November
1016, his reign cut
short after he was
caught short.

HENRY II

KING HENRY'S ANNOYANCE INCREASED WHEN CROSSED BY A TURBULENT PRIEST. HIS KNIGHTS OVERHEARD A REQUEST FOR A MURDER AND SO THOMAS BECKET DECEASED.

Henry's mother was the English Matilda, but his father was Geoffrey of Anjou, and he inherited about half of France, so he was well placed to bring the two countries together again. But Henry also asserted control over Wales, took a piece of Ireland, and forced the Scottish king to recognise him as his superior.

Meanwhile he tried to assert the rule of law in England, by which he meant the king's law, not the church's. Naturally the church wasn't keen on that. And even when he installed his pal Thomas Becket as Archbishop of Canterbury, the chap had the cheek to disagree with the king!

The story goes that Henry didn't mean Tommy B to die, he just expressed some mild frustration within the hearing of some of his knights, who, overeager to please the king, ran off to Canterbury Cathedral and killed the knave in the nave.

Henry II

Ruled England and western France, 1154–1189.
King because Stephen promised his mother Matilda he could be.
First language French.   **Family** Plantagenet.

ELEANOR OF AQUITAINE

THERE WAS A FRENCH QUEEN KNOWN AS ELEANOR,
STRONG-WILLED — THERE WAS REALLY NO TELLIN' 'ER.
SHE EGGED ON HER LAD
TO CHALLENGE HIS DAD,
WHO JAILED HER, INSTEAD OF EXPELLIN' 'ER.

Eleanor was not a ruling monarch as such, but was more powerful than many kings who ruled in their own right. She went off crusading with her first husband King Louis VII of France, but decided pretty quickly he was boring, moaning: 'I have married a monk.' Eventually she managed to get the marriage annulled.

Eleanor, now 30, sent a message to her 19-year-old cousin, Henry of Normandy, proposing they get together. As luck would have it, a year after they married he succeeded to the English throne as Henry II.

The power couple had eight children, but fell out, as so many couples do, over child-rearing. The king felt it was a bit naughty of little Henry to raise an army against daddy, but Eleanor said it was fine as long as he let his brothers Richard and John join in. Henry felt a bit betrayed by this, and imprisoned her for 16 years.

Eleanor of Aquitaine

Ruled Duchess of Aquitaine, 1137–1204; Queen Consort of France, 1137–1152, England 1154–1189. **Queen because** Married Louis VII of France and Henry II of England. **First language** French. **Age at accession** 15.

FREDERICK BARBAROSSA

THERE WAS AN OLD FELLOW NAMED FRED
WHOSE BEARD WAS EXCEEDINGLY RED,
HE CONQUERED MILAN
BY MAKING EACH MAN
BITE FIGS FROM MULE'S BOTTOMS, IT'S SAID.

Frederick I, known as Barbarossa ('red-beard'), ruled large parts of Europe in the back half of the 12th century – but not without a certain amount of effort on his part. He could be diplomatic, handing out land to nobles and kissing the Pope's ring when required. But he was also not above razing recalcitrant cities to the ground.

In 1162, as legend has it, he left his wife Beatrice in Milan, where she was badly treated by being made to ride backwards on a mule or an ass. That may not sound so bad, but his revenge was.

Right, said Fred: you Milanese chaps, come here. And he made each of them pluck a fig from a mule's backside with his teeth. From which, it is claimed, derives the Italian insulting gesture called 'ficus' or fig – which consists of putting one's thumb between one's index and middle fingers.

Frederick Barbarossa

Ruled Holy Roman Empire (Germany, Italy, Burgundy), 1155–1190.
Emperor because Elected by the princes of the empire. **Cause of death** Drowned on the way to crusade. **Legacy** A rude gesture.

RICHARD I

KING RICHARD THE LIONHEART'S REIGN
WAS MOSTLY SPENT FIGHTING IN VAIN
THE SARACEN HORDE;
BACK HERE HE WAS BORED,
AND RATHER FED UP WITH THE RAIN.

Richard I managed to get fantastic PR for his 'Lionheart' brand. He spent most of his time on crusades, trying to capture Jerusalem from the Muslim forces of Saladin and massacring prisoners now and then. This endeared him to the monks of the old media, and also to the new media – the minstrels who spread songs of his bold deeds across Europe.

This great English king only visited Britain briefly to moan about the weather and drum up funds for his next crusade. As well as imposing heavy taxes, he gave Scotland back to the Scots in exchange for 10,000 silver marks, and said he would have sold London had there been a buyer.

On the way back from one crusade he was shipwrecked and captured by the Austrians. The ransom, which left Britain bankrupt, was organised by his mum, Eleanor, whom he had released from his father's prison to run the country in his absence.

Richard I

Ruled England and France, 1189–1199. **King because** His dad Henry was, and his big brother Henry died. **First language** French.
Cause of death Gangrene after being shot with a crossbow in France.

JOHN

ACCEDING TO POWER, KING JOHN
FOUND MOST OF HIS EMPIRE WAS GONE,
BUT HIS CHARTER OF RIGHTS,
AGREED WITH THE KNIGHTS,
FIVE HUNDRED YEARS LATER LIVES ON.

John's first act on becoming king was to have his French nephew Arthur killed, which so annoyed the French side of the family that he promptly lost most of the family lands there – keeping only Aquitaine (parts of which, like the Dordogne, are still pretty English today, but for other reasons).

So having spent most of Richard's reign in France trying to raise money and armies to invade England, he now found himself as king trying to raise money and armies to invade France.

But making friends and influencing people wasn't John's strong suit, and in the end the barons got so fed up they made him sign Magna Carta, giving them all kinds of rights. John immediately said he was only kidding, so the barons got France to invade again. But, just in the nick of time, John died. And Magna Carta lived.

John

Ruled England and Aquitaine, 1199–1216.
King because His dad Henry was, and his brother Richard died.
Achievements Magna Carta (through gritted teeth).
Nickname John Lackland.

LLEWELYN THE GREAT

LLEWELYN OF GWYNEDD, THE GREAT, FOUGHT HARD TO CREATE A WELSH STATE. AT HOME THERE WAS STRIFE WHEN LLEW FOUND HIS WIFE IN BED WITH BLACK WILLIAM, HIS MATE.

Prince Llewelyn ap Iorwerth took over as ruler of Gwynedd aged 18, and at various points made peace and fought wars with King John and King Henry III of England, during the course of which he expanded his control over most of Wales. In 1205 he married John's daughter Joan.

Llewelyn had a troubled friendship with an Anglo-Norman lord named William de Braose, known by the Welsh as Black William. In 1230 they decided to make up by marrying their son to William's daughter. Unfortunately, William and Joan got a bit too close while discussing the table settings, and Llewelyn found them together in the bedchamber.

William was hanged in punishment – but it all ended happily ever after, as the wedding went ahead anyway. Well, it would have been a shame to cancel it after they'd bought all that food, and when everyone was looking forward to the big day.

Llewelyn the Great

Ruled Gwynedd, North Wales, 1200–1240; most of Wales, 1218–1240.
King because His grandfather Owain ruled Gwynedd; the rest he conquered.
First language Welsh.   **Achievements** Built lots of castles.

HENRY III

KING HENRY WAS CAUGHT UNAWARES
BY BARONS DEMANDING THEIR SHARES
OF GOVERNING POWER,
WHILE HE FILLED THE TOWER
WITH LIONS AND TIGERS AND BEARS!

King Henry was only nine when he took power. So as a kid he was able to see clearly what was wrong with England – there was no zoo for your parents to take you to!

Other kings weren't sure what to get him as a present, so they gave him animals – he got an elephant from King Louis IX of France, a polar bear from King Haakon of Norway and three lions from Frederick III, to match his England football shirt.

He also had Westminster Abbey renovated, and a great hall built next to it which served as a bear pit of a different kind – the barons found it a useful venue to hold parliaments, where they demanded more say in things like raising taxes to pay for wars.

Henry III

Ruled England and Aquitaine, 1216–1272.
King because His dad John was. **First language** French.
Achievements Created parliament (accidentally).

EDWARD I

ED LONGSHANKS OUTLAWED PROSTITUTION,
WHILE JEWS SUFFERED HARSH PERSECUTION
AND SCOTLAND WAS HAMMERED —
HE WASN'T ENAMOURED
OF WHAT WE NOW CALL DEVOLUTION.

Edward I was called Edward Longshanks because he was tall. He liked picking fights with the neighbours, especially Wales and Scotland. His armies fought William Wallace and Robert the Bruce, violently and frequently suppressing their attempts to keep Scotland independent, only to see another rebellion start up.

But it wasn't just the Scots he had it in for. In 1275 Edward introduced a law requiring Jews to wear a yellow Star of David – as repeated by the Nazis more than 600 years later. Then in 1290 he went a step further and expelled them from the country altogether, allowing him to confiscate their money to pay for more wars.

Edward also launched his own war on vice, kicking London's prostitutes out of the city. So of course they just set up shop over the river in Southwark, creating an Amsterdam-style tolerated red-light district on the South Bank.

Edward I

Ruled England and Wales, 1272–1307. **King because** His dad Henry was.
Legacy Heightened anti-English sentiment in Scotland.
Cause of death Dysentery, while campaigning.

EDWARD II

KING EDWARD PREFERRED HIS OWN KIND
FOR WHICH HE WAS SOMEWHAT MALIGNED.
THE FELLOW HE LOVED
WAS KILLED, THEN THEY SHOVED
A POKER UP EDWARD'S BEHIND.

Edward II has had a uniformly bad press. This is partly because where his father was a 'hammer of the Scots', he was more like the nail – repeatedly losing in battle. But it was mainly because of his relationship with his 'favourite', i.e. lover, Piers Gaveston. Piers upset the barons whose support Edward needed – whether because he was obnoxious, or because they were homophobic, or just jealous, who knows? They kept making Edward banish Piers, but he kept coming back, so in the end they murdered him.

Piers was married to Isabella, daughter of the French King Philip IV, but more or less the only thing they agreed on was that they both liked sleeping with men. Isabella and her lover Richard Mortimer conspired with the barons to overthrow Edward. They tortured him in Berkeley Castle, and stuck a red-hot poker stuck up his backside – a horrible way to die, but one that shows no marks, so his death could be presented as a mystery.

Edward II

Ruled England and Wales, 1307–1327. **King because** His dad Edward was. **First language** French. **Cause of death** Mysterious – but might have had something to do with the poker.

ROBERT THE BRUCE

THE SCOTTISH KING ROBERT THE BRUCE
WAS WONDERING WHAT WAS THE USE,
THEN ONE SMALL ARACHNID
INSPIRED — THOUGH IT'S HACKNEYED —
THE FEATS HE WENT ON TO PRODUCE.

Robert the Bruce spent a lot of his time intriguing against other claimants for the crown of Scotland, and no sooner had he been crowned at Scone than he faced a civil war as well as one with the English (no doubt started by a dispute over how to pronounce Scone), and was forced into exile.

While hiding, he's famously supposed to have been inspired to return to the fight by a spider that kept on trying to rebuild its web. Equally likely is that he found a copy of the ancient Chinese general Sun Tzu's *The Art of War*, and realised guerrilla resistance was the way forward.

Either way, he returned to Scotland and turned the war against the English, led by the ineffectual Edward II. At Bannockburn Bruce's outnumbered forces sent 'proud Edward's army... homeward – tae think again' – as Scottish sports fans still sing.

Robert the Bruce
Ruled Scotland, 1306–1329.
King because His ancestor David was, and he defeated his rivals.
Languages Gaelic, Scots and French.   **Cause of death** Leprosy.

EDWARD III

KING EDWARD LIKED FIGHTING IN FRANCE
WHERE LONGBOWS GAVE ENGLAND A CHANCE;
THE USE OF THE ARCHER,
A MAJOR DEPARTURE,
PREVENTING A GALLIC ADVANCE.

Ah, Crécy... where the victorious English longbowmen gloriously beat the French. Well, that is true. But, to put things in perspective, although Edward III's father was English(-ish), his mother was French, and he thought he should have been King of France too. Hence the Hundred Years' War.

Edward succeeded where previous kings had failed by getting the nobles onside. He created more earldoms and dukedoms than you could shake a lance at, organised jousting tournaments for them and set up the Most Noble Order of the Garter, supposedly named after a Countess's dropped garter which the king chivalrously picked up for her. The order still exists, although in 700-odd years no one's worked out what it's for.

Having become king at 14 because his mum had his dad murdered, he then got rid of her lover Mortimer three years later and packed Mum off to a nunnery. Who says chivalry's dead?

Edward III

Ruled England and Wales, 1327–1377; parts of northern France from 1346.
King because His dad Edward was.   **High point** Beating the French at Crécy.
Low point Black Death killing half the population.

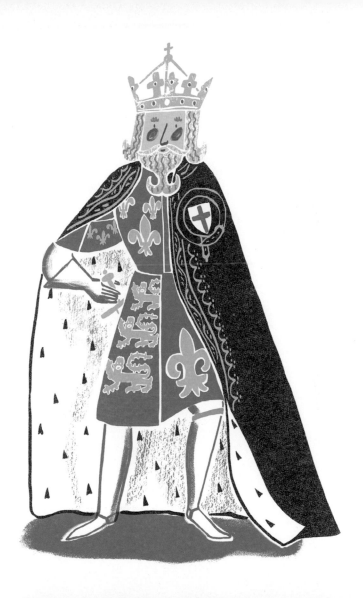

RICHARD II

THERE WAS A YOUNG MAN FROM BORDEAUX
WHOSE NOSE WAS IN NEED OF A BLOW,
SO SOME PEOPLE RECKONED
THAT RICHARD THE SECOND
WAS FIRST TO GIVE HANKIES A GO.

Though born in France, Richard of Bordeaux spoke English well enough to converse with the common man. When the peasants revolted, he told them their demands would be met, then said, 'Ha-ha, only joking,' and had all the ringleaders killed.

He was still only 15, but this left him convinced that he was God's gift to the world, with a divine right to rule. So he got into disputes with parliament, the Irish, the French and anyone else who disagreed. Eventually he was overthrown by Henry Bolingbroke, who persuaded him to abdicate, then left him to starve in Pontefract Castle.

But he left as a legacy a court obsessed with new fashions, such as absurdly long toes on slippers and baggy sleeves. And so he wouldn't have to wipe the royal nose on those elegant sleeves, he had the royal tailor knock out some square pieces of cloth called handkerchiefs.

Richard II

Ruled England and Wales, 1377–1399.
King because His grandad Edward was (and outlived his dad, Edward).
Age at accession 10. **Cause of death** Starvation.

HENRY IV

WHEN HENRY THE NEW KING WAS CROWNED
AN OMINOUS PORTENT WAS FOUND,
FOR, SO IT IS SAID,
UNEASY THE HEAD
ON WHICH MANY HEADLICE ABOUND.

Henry Bolingbroke had a weak claim to the throne, which he made up for with a strong show of force, invading while Richard was off in Ireland.

This meant even more people than usual disputed his right to rule, and even he had his doubts, according to Shakespeare, who summed up his precarious position with the line: 'Uneasy lies the head that wears a crown'.

Everyone was on the lookout for portents to show there was something wrong with his being king, like when one of the witnesses at his coronation said his head was crawling with lice. Even his death of a horrible skin complaint, with a massive tumour under his nose, was taken as evidence that God was not happy with him.

Henry IV

Ruled England and (some of the time) Wales, 1399–1413.
King because His grandad Edward was (and he forced Richard II out).
Born Lincolnshire. **Family** Lancaster.

CHARLES VI OF FRANCE

KING CHARLES WAS AS MAD AS A HATTER,
BELIEVING HIS BODILY MATTER
WAS MADE OUT OF GLASS
OF SUCH A FINE CLASS,
IF TOUCHED, HE MIGHT SUDDENLY SHATTER.

His father, Charles V, was known as Charles the Wise, his uncle was Philip the Bold, and his cousin was John the Fearless. But Charles VI was to go down in history as Charles the Mad. It must have driven him round the bend.

Charles's first recorded episode of insanity involved mistaking his own knights for assassins and killing four of them. At various points he was unable to recognise his wife and thought he was St George, and at one point he refused to wash for five months.

Perhaps he just didn't have the right non-smear cleaning product – because the weirdest manifestation of Charles's madness was a condition known as glass delusion. The king wore reinforced clothing and would not let anyone touch him for fear he would break into pieces. But most people saw through this, realising he was just a bit cracked.

Charles VI of France

Ruled France, 1380–1422.
King because His dad Charles was.   **Age at accession** 11.
Nickname Charles the Mad.

OWAIN GLYNDWR

THERE WAS A WELSH RULER NAMED OWEN
WHO VANISHED, WHICH MEANS THERE'S NO KNOWIN'
IF HE DIED SWORD IN HAND
DEFENDING HIS LAND
OR IF — AS SOME SAY — HE'S STILL GOIN'.

Owain Glyndwr, or Owen Glendower as he was called by the English, refused to accept their imperialistic insistence that he put some proper vowels in his name. As hereditary Prince of Powys, he led a revolt against English rule in the beginning of the 15th century, succeeding in uniting various Welsh factions under his leadership and getting the backing of France.

In 1404 he was crowned Prince of Wales – the last proper one before it became just a title for the English king's eldest son. But the English held on to a number of castles, and eventually managed to crush the rebellion.

Owen was last sighted in 1412, and was never captured, leading to many legends that he kept going for years afterwards. Though probably not 600 of them, to be fair, so it's unlikely he will return to lead the Welsh struggle for freedom now.

Owain Glyndwr

Ruled Wales, 1400–1415-ish.
Prince because His dad was Prince of Powys, and he fought for the rest.
First language Welsh. **Legacy** Services to Welsh legend.

HENRY V

KING HENRY THE FIFTH TOOK HIS CHANCE
TO LEAD ENGLAND'S NOBLE ADVANCE,
ALTHOUGH IF THERE'S TRUTH
IN TALES OF HIS YOUTH,
THE WINE MAY HAVE DRAWN HIM TO FRANCE.

Henry V's public image owes an awful lot to Shakespeare's portrayal of the hell-raising, hard-drinking, womanising teen who turned into a charismatic warrior king. His military campaign was helped by the French being split between warring factions, Burgundy and Armagnac – both coincidentally among Henry's favourite tipples in his youth.

His most famous victory was at Agincourt, where the heroic tale of outnumbered British archers is only slightly undercut by Henry's war crime in ordering all the prisoners to be killed. Henry was also notable for his ability to address the troops in English, as at the siege of Harfleur, where Shakespeare has him exhorting the troops: 'Once more unto the breach, dear friends, once more/Or close the wall up with our English dead'. As a motivational speech it seems to have worked, but one-third of his troops did indeed die – of dysentery, which was eventually to kill him too.

Henry V

Ruled England and Wales, northern France, 1413–1422.
King because His dad Henry was.
Family Lancaster.   **Cause of death** Dysentery.

HENRY VI

WHEN HENRY THE FIFTH HAD STOPPED BREATHING
HIS NINE-MONTH-OLD HEIR WAS STILL TEETHING.
A KING IN A NAPPY
MADE RIVALS UNHAPPY,
WITH RICHARD OF YORK SIMPLY SEETHING.

Henry VI became king aged nine months – his skull had barely joined
up, so they waited until he was eight to crown him. He also became
King of France under a deal reached after Agincourt between his father
Henry V and his maternal grandfather Charles the Mad.

Over the next few decades, however, the home side (France) finally
won the Hundred Years' War, leaving England with only Calais as
a continental base, and apparently prompting a year-long mental
breakdown in Henry (who may have inherited a psychiatric condition
from his grandfather).

No sooner was the Hundred Years' War over than the Wars of the
Roses began, when Richard of York – acting on the maxim 'don't get
mad, get angry' – challenged the increasingly unstable Henry for the
throne. Although Richard was defeated and killed, his son Edward
overthrew Henry in 1461.

Henry VI

Ruled England and Wales, 1422–1461 (and again 1470–1471); France,
1422–1453. **King because** His dad Henry was.
Age at accession Too young.   **Family** Lancaster.

EDWARD IV

THE WHITE ROSE DEFEATED THE RED,
PRODUCING ANOTHER KING ED;
ALL VERY HISTORIC,
ALTHOUGH BRIEFLY WARWICK
PUT HENRY THE SIXTH BACK INSTEAD.

The name 'Wars of the Roses' was only coined centuries later to describe the fight for succession between rival claimants from the Houses of York (symbol: white rose) and Lancaster (symbol: red rose).

Although Edward defeated Henry in round one, there were a lot of shifting allegiances among the nobles, most notably Warwick the Kingmaker, who decided in 1470 to unmake King Edward and remake the ousted King Henry. In round two, Edward reappeared and secured a 2–0 aggregate victory.

While Edward's death was unexciting, he made sure his brother George's was more exotic, having him executed for treason by being drowned in a barrel of Malmsey, a rather sweet variety of wine.

Edward IV

Ruled England and Wales, 1461–1470 and 1471–1483.
King because His army defeated Henry's.
House York.   **Cause of death** Natural causes, amazingly.

EDWARD V

KING EDWARD THE FIFTH, THE POOR FLOWER, WAS JUST ON THE THRESHOLD OF POWER WHEN RICHARD PLANTAGENET — CAN YOU IMAGINE IT? — PUT HIM TO DEATH IN THE TOWER.

Although he got to be called Edward V, little Ed is better remembered as one of the two princes – along with his kid brother Richard – believed to have been killed by their uncle, guardian and – as it happens – successor, Richard III.

He never even got crowned in fact, so really was king in name only. Richard was babysitting at the time of the sad disappearance of the two brothers, so although their bodies were never found, he clearly had questions to answer.

Edward V

Ruled Nowhere, to be honest. **King because** His dad Edward was.
Age at accession/death 12. **Cause of death** Missing presumed killed by Richard III.

RICHARD III

YOU SHOULDN'T BELIEVE WHAT YOU'VE HEARD ABOUT POOR OLD RICHARD THE THIRD; THOUGH SHAKESPEARE CONVINCES THAT HE KILLED THE PRINCES WE DON'T REALLY KNOW WHAT OCCURRED.

OK, let's hear the other side of the story.

If Richard III did kill his nephews, it may have been because of a shrewd suspicion they'd do the same to him given half a chance. You could say he had a hunch.

Or did he? For centuries, historians have debated the truth or otherwise of Shakespeare's portrait of the wicked hunchback who killed his poor nephews in the Tower of London. His defenders argued that it was all Tudor propaganda. And after all, no body, no murder.

Richard died at Bosworth in 1485, the last English king killed in battle. When his body was dug up in 2012 underneath a municipal car park in Leicester, scientists confirmed their own hunch that Richard did indeed have a form of scoliosis, or curvature of the spine. Not that that makes him a killer, of course.

Richard III

Ruled England and Wales, 1483–1485.
King because His brother Edward was.
Cause of death Battling. **Legacy** Services to car parking.

VLAD THE IMPALER

ROMANIA'S VLAD THE IMPALER WAS KNOWN AS A FLOGGER AND FLAILER, AMBITIOUS, MALICIOUS, CAPRICIOUS AND VICIOUS, A BURNER AND BOILER AND NAILER.

I'm sure Vlad Dracul had his good points – maybe he was kind to animals? (No, apparently not.)

He was kidnapped by the Ottoman Sultan as a child, but by all accounts he was treated pretty well then. So there's really no excuse for some of the stuff he did later – like nailing the Sultan's ambassadors' heads to their turbans. Or inviting all the local nobles to a feast, then rounding them up and forcing him to build them a castle, before impaling the survivors. Or boiling and burning people alive.

Perhaps the one thing you could say in Vlad's favour is that there is no evidence that he was an undead bloodsucker – Bram Stoker just borrowed the name and Vlad's grisly image when creating Count Dracula.

Vlad the Impaler

Ruled Wallachia, 1456–1462 (with gaps).
Prince because His dad Vlad was.
Legacy Services to vampire tourism.

HENRY VII

YOUNG HENRY THE SEVENTH FROM WALES
DID NOT INSPIRE WARRIOR TALES,
PREFERRING ACCOUNTS,
HE MADE LARGE AMOUNTS
WITH TREATIES TO BOOST EXPORT SALES.

Having defeated Richard and seized the crown by force, Henry Tudor had a surprisingly peaceful reign – relatively, anyway.

He had to fight off the odd pretender challenging his rule, but broke away from the long-standing tradition of fighting Scotland and France at every opportunity – perhaps being Welsh made him less bothered about such petty rivalries. He also signed a treaty with the Netherlands to allow England's growing export trade in wool to flourish.

He wasn't averse to imprisoning and torturing nobles who opposed him, but generally found a more effective tool was to tax them heavily. This had the useful side effect of making him exceedingly rich, but made him profoundly unsuitable for romantic tales and songs: 'The Ballad of the Bold Tax Collector' was never going to be a winner.

Henry VII

Ruled England and Wales, 1485–1509.
King because He was the last Lancastrian left standing when Richard III was defeated. **Age at accession** 28. **Family** Plantagenet/Tudor.

HENRY VIII

SIX TIMES HENRY TUDOR GOT WED,
UNHAPPY WITH HOW HIS WIVES BRED,
AND WHEN THINGS TURNED SOUR,
EXPLOITING HIS POWER
HE SHOUTED OUT, 'OFF WITH HER HEAD!'

Henry VIII only actually had *two* of his wives beheaded – let's not exaggerate. One died in childbirth, two he divorced and one lucky wife outlived him. But in the days before the quickie divorce, Henry needed a papal dispensation. And when the Pope said 'Nope', it led to a rather more serious split – between the Church of England and the Catholic Church. There being no ecclesiastical prenup, Henry played hardball when it came to dividing up the Church's property, dissolving the monasteries and taking their land – all the Pope was left with was the record collection.

All this came about because Henry desperately wanted a legitimate son. Wife No. 2, Anne Boleyn, was tried for adultery, incest and treason, but her real crime was producing a daughter. Jane Seymour then gave him a boy-child, but died a fortnight after giving birth. So he repeated the whole marrying, divorcing, beheading game until Catherine Parr survived him.

Henry VIII

Ruled England, Wales and Ireland, 1509–1547. **King because** His dad Henry was. **Cause of death** Diabetes, morbid obesity, genetic disorder... take your pick. **Legacy** The Church of England and divorce.

IVAN THE TERRIBLE

OLD IVAN KILLED FOLKS HERE AND THERE AND MURDERED HIS OWN SON AND HEIR, BUT MOST THINK THE TSAR WENT THAT BIT TOO FAR BY USING THE SKIN OF A BEAR.

Ivan's nickname is usually rendered in English as 'the Terrible', but a more accurate translation might be 'Terrifying'. Ivan certainly inspired fear. When he thought Russian nobles from Novgorod were plotting against him, he sent in his army of secret police and slaughtered them. They didn't try that again.

Ivan killed his own son and heir more in the heat of the moment, in an argument. Perhaps he was lucky – as Ivan the Terrible got madder he came up with more and more grotesque ways of killing his perceived enemies. Boiling alive, impaling and blowing up on a barrel of gunpowder all featured.

But the crowning glory was the punishment meted out to the Archbishop of Novgorod, who was sewn into a bearskin and hunted by a pack of hounds. That's pretty terrible.

Ivan the Terrible

Ruled Russia, 1533–1584.
Tsar because Dad was Grand Prince.
Age at accession 3.

EDWARD VI

KING EDWARD WAS NEXT IN THE LINE
AND SO HE TOOK POWER AGED NINE,
HE HAD TO LEAVE SCHOOL
IN ORDER TO RULE
AND IMPLEMENT CRANMER'S DESIGN.

Considering Edward spent his adolescence on the throne and died aged 15, quite a lot happened during his reign – or on his watch, anyway.

Edward was the first actual Protestant king, and was closely advised by his Archbishop of Canterbury Thomas Cranmer, and the Lord Protector John Dudley, no friends of Rome. Edward was quick to consolidate the new religion, breaking with the Pope by introducing services in English and letting priests marry.

He was a sickly child, but not having a father or mother to write a note to say he was too sick to rule today, he just had to get on with it. And it turned out he really *was* ill – he died of tuberculosis.

Edward VI

Ruled England, Wales and Ireland, 1547–1553.
King because His dad Henry was.
Religion Protestant. **Mother** Jane Seymour.

JANE GREY

THE NEXT ONE IN POWER, QUEEN JANE,
WAS NOT VERY LONG TO REMAIN,
A BRIEF PASSING PHASE,
NO MORE THAN NINE DAYS,
A SHOWER, NOT REALLY A REIGN.

Lady Jane Grey was a bit of an unexpected choice for queen – Henry VIII's Act of Succession had made clear that, after Edward, his daughters Mary and Elizabeth were next in line. But Edward VI was persuaded to rip this up and nominate his Protestant cousin Jane to stop Catholic Mary. Well, she was Henry VII's great-granddaughter, after all!

They say a week is a long time in politics, but Jane barely had time to get measured for her ceremonial robes before an outraged Mary declared herself the true queen, with the support of the lords who made up the Privy Council.

Jane was deposed and locked up in the Tower, arrested, and executed the following year – having refused to give up her Protestant faith.

Jane Grey

Ruled Her own bedroom, 10–19 July, 1553.
Queen because She was Edward's first cousin once removed.
Cause of death Execution.   **Achievements** Getting through the weekend.

MARY I

THE QUEEN WHO WAS CALLED BLOODY MARY
MADE PROTESTANTS' LIVES PRETTY HAIRY:
THEY HAD TO FORSAKE
THEIR FAITH, OR THE STAKE
AWAITED — A LITTLE BIT SCARY.

Mary was the daughter of Henry VIII and his first wife, Catherine of Aragon. She had been brought up Catholic, and swiftly restored England to the fold – suddenly, Latin mass was back, married priests had to be single again, and please could the monasteries have their land back?

That last one was a bit difficult, but Mary pressed on with trying to reverse the Reformation, by insisting Protestants renounce their faith or be killed as heretics. About 300 were burned at the stake, including Archbishop Cranmer.

Mary married Prince Philip of Spain and was keen to produce an heir, but Broody Mary was unable to conceive. In 1554 it seemed that the queen regnant was pregnant, but just when everyone was getting ready for the royal baby shower, it went away. She died a few years later.

Mary I
Ruled England, Wales and Ireland, 1553–1558.
Queen because Her dad Henry was king. **Age at accession** 37.
Religion Catholic.

ELIZABETH I

IT'S SAID GOOD QUEEN BESS DIED A VIRGIN,
UNMARRIED, DESPITE PHILIP'S URGIN'.
HE SENT AN ARMADA
TO SHOW HER HIS ARDOUR
BUT SAW ALL HIS WARSHIPS SUBMERGIN'.

You wait centuries for a female ruler, then three come along at once! The difference with Elizabeth was she stayed the course – though, like Jane and Mary, she was unable to leave an heir.

Elizabeth rejected her brother-in-law Philip's proposal, but it was probably more general political and religious rivalry that was behind his attempt to invade in 1588. Coming from sunny Spain, he failed to take the weather forecast seriously, and the Armada was defeated by a big storm.

Under Elizabeth, England once more broke with the Pope, although Bess favoured a less hardline interpretation of Protestantism that kept some of the nice music and things. But life still got tough for committed Catholics, especially after the Pope called her a heretic – more than 100 priests were executed under laws designed to stop Catholicism spreading.

Elizabeth I

Ruled England, Wales and Ireland, 1558–1603.
Queen because Her dad Henry was.
Mother Anne Boleyn. **Religion** Protestant.

GRACE O'MALLEY

AN IRISH CLAN CHIEFTAIN NAMED GRACE
SAILED IN TO MEET BESS FACE TO FACE,
THEY CAME TO A DEAL
BUT GRACE DIDN'T KNEEL —
SHE WOULDN'T ACCEPT SECOND PLACE.

Grace O'Malley (Gráinne Ní Mháille in Irish) has been called the Sea Queen of Connacht, and enjoyed a ruler's privilege of taxation over shipping. But as far as the English were concerned, she was a pirate. English monarchs from King John onwards had claimed lordship over Ireland, but in practice only held sway over a small area, the rest being ruled by independent nobles or clan chieftains like the O'Malleys. But since Henry VIII had declared himself King of Ireland in 1542, England was increasingly enforcing its rule.

When Grace's two sons and her brother-in-law were captured by the English governor Sir John Bingham, she sailed to Greenwich Palace in London to confront Queen Elizabeth as one queen to another. They came to an agreement whereby Grace would stop backing rebellions against English rule, and Elizabeth would recall Bingham and release her family members.

Grace O'Malley

Ruled Connacht, 1560s–1603.
Queen because Her dad Eoghan was king.
First language Irish.

MARY, QUEEN OF SCOTS

QUEEN MARY, THE QUEEN OF THE SCOTS,
GOT INTO SOME DIFFICULT SPOTS,
ESCAPING THE RAP
FOR KILLING HER CHAP
BUT SENTENCED FOR JOINING IN PLOTS.

Mary Queen of Scots was basically French. Crowned when she had barely learned to focus, she then spent most of her childhood in France and married a French prince. She returned to rule Scotland aged 18 when her husband died, but found she was now the wrong religion, as most people had become Protestant.

Overthrown and kicked out of Scotland, she went to see her cousin Elizabeth, who put her up in a series of country houses. Perhaps like in Cluedo, Liz had to get Mary into the billiard room to establish whether she had plotted to kill her second husband, as most people suspected.

In the end, it wasn't the murder rap that got her, it was her involvement in a succession of plots to kill Elizabeth and take her place as Queen of England. Or perhaps she would have been called Mary, Queen of English.

Mary, Queen of Scots

Ruled Scotland, 1542–1567.
Queen because Her dad James was king.
Age at accession 6 days. **Religion** Catholic.

JAMES I
(JAMES VI OF SCOTLAND)

THE PROTESTANT MONARCH, KING JAMES,
ESCAPED BEING BLOWN UP IN FLAMES
BY GUY FAWKES, A FELLER
WITH BOMBS IN A CELLAR
AND UNPARLIAMENTARY AIMS.

King James was made King of Scotland as a baby when his mother Mary was forced to abdicate. But once he got the chance to rule England too, he hot-footed it to London and only went back north once. His desire to cement his rule of England, Scotland and Ireland had a big impact on relations between the nations of the British Isles for the next few centuries.

But it almost finished not long after his accession in England. In 1605, a Catholic named Guy Fawkes was found in a rented cellar underneath parliament on the eve of the state opening, with enough gunpowder to blow the whole place sky-high. The funny thing is, James hated having to compromise with parliament so much he'd probably have helped blow it up as long as he wasn't inside at the time!

James I/VI

Ruled Scotland 1567–1625; England, Wales and Ireland, 1603–1625.
King because His mother Mary was queen (Scotland); his great-great-grandfather Henry VII was king (the rest).   **Age at accession** 13 months.
Religion Protestant.

MINI-MONARCHS
KIDS IN CROWNS

6 days

MARY, QUEEN OF SCOTS

She'd barely drawn breath.

9 months

HENRY VI

Was running the country before he could walk.

13 months

JAMES I/VI

No sooner had he started to talk than he had to give orders.

3 years

IVAN THE TERRIBLE

He never got over the terrible twos.

9 years

HENRY III

Became king just after his ninth birthday to edge in ahead of Edward VI, who was all of 9¼.

CHARLES I

KING CHARLES THOUGHT HIS RIGHT WAS DIVINE,
ALL PART OF THE LORD'S GRAND DESIGN,
BUT WAR AGAINST PARLIAMENT
SADLY FOR CHARLIE MEANT
PUTTING HIS NECK ON THE LINE.

Charles I believed kings had a divine right to rule, and he didn't like parliament interfering. But having stopped parliament from sitting, he couldn't raise taxes the normal way, so he had to use all kinds of methods of extortion instead.

Meanwhile, people in Scotland and Ireland rebelled against English rule, so Charles went back to parliament, floppy hat in hand, to ask for some money, but they told him to take a running jump.

The ensuing civil war was won by the parliamentarians, who chopped Charles's head off – suggesting maybe God wasn't on his side after all.

Charles I

Ruled England, Wales, Scotland, Ireland, 1625–1649.
King because His dad James was.   **Religion** High-church Protestant.
Cause of death Decapitation.

WAY TO GO
WEIRDEST ROYAL DEATHS

HENRY I

SURFEIT OF LAMPREYS

He didn't know when to stop. Or just not start.

EDMUND IRONSIDE

STABBED WHILE ON TOILET

Just when he thought he'd get a moment's peace.

GEORGE I

SURFEIT OF STRAWBERRIES

There's something they're not telling us – it was the cream, right?

GEORGE II

DRINKING COCOA ON THE TOILET

Judgement on him for such depraved behaviour!

WILLIAM III

HORSE TRIPPED ON MOLEHILL

As a symbol of royal mortality, it takes some beating.

OLIVER CROMWELL

THE NEW LORD PROTECTOR, OLD NOLL,
SOON RIPPED UP THE OLD PROTOCOL,
HIS PURITAN RULE
MEANT NO MARKING YULE,
NO SEX PLEASE, AND NO ALCOHOL.

Oliver Cromwell was in charge of the army that defeated Charles I,
so it was only natural he should take over – well, no one was arguing,
anyway.

Although Britain now no longer had a king, he continued the royal
tradition of brutally suppressing rebellions across the British Isles,
especially in Ireland, where his religious fervour made the massacres of
Catholics bloodier than ever.

As a theocratic military dictator, he proceeded to arrest
parliamentarians who disagreed with him, and clamp down on
immorality. Adultery carried a death sentence, enforced by Taliban-style
morality police, and trivial pursuits like sport, theatres, pubs and the
celebration of Christmas were banned – the kind of laws you'd struggle
to get past an elected parliament.

Oliver Cromwell

Ruled England, Wales, Scotland, Ireland, 1649–1660.
Lord Protector because The Parliamentarians won the Civil War.
Religion Very puritanical Protestant.

CHARLES II

THE MERRY KING CHARLES WAS RESTORED
BUT MATTERS OF STATE LEFT HIM BORED;
PREFERRING TO SIN
WITH ACTRESS NELL GWYNN,
HE GAMBLED AND HUNTED AND WHORED.

When Cromwell died, his son Richard was unable to cut it as Lord Protector, so with a bit of gentle persuasion from the army, parliament agreed to have a king again. Charles II, nicknamed the Merry Monarch, wasted no time reversing all the puritan edicts and bringing back theatre, sports and debauchery of all sorts. Women were even allowed to act in plays!

He had a string of mistresses, most famously the actress and orange-seller Nell Gwynn, and fathered a dozen or so children by them.

Although he denied being a Catholic, he had secretly promised his cousin King Louis XIV of France that he would become one, and duly converted on his deathbed. Apparently Charles took four days to die, but he probably needed all that and more for his confession!

Charles II

Ruled England, Wales, Scotland, Ireland, 1660–1685.
King because His dad Charles I was.
Religion Protestant, veering Catholic.   **Cause of death** Apoplexy.

JAMES II

KING JAMES WAS ACCUSED OF DECEPTION
REGARDING HIS BOY-CHILD'S CONCEPTION.
ALTHOUGH MANY QUERY
THE WARMING-PAN THEORY,
IT ALTERED HIS PUBLIC PERCEPTION.

King James II's big problem was that he was a Catholic king in a very anti-Catholic country. Before he came to the throne there had been strenuous efforts to change the rules and bar Catholics from the succession – parliament even passed a bill urging that his marriage to the 15-year-old Italian Catholic Mary of Modena not be consummated.

When it was, and she bore a son, the rumour went round that the child was not his, and/or not hers, and had in fact been smuggled into her bedchamber in a warming-pan.

In order to ensure a Protestant succession, a group of his enemies invited Mary (James's daughter from his first marriage) and her husband William of Orange to take over. James took one look at the size of William's army and fled to France, dropping the Great Seal of the Realm in the Thames.

James II
Ruled England, Wales, Scotland, Ireland, 1685–1688.
King because His dad Charles I was.
Age at accession 52. **Religion** Catholic.

WILLIAM III AND MARY II

THOUGH NOT THE SUCCESSOR AS SUCH,
BILL WANTED TO RULE VERY MUCH;
SINCE MARY HAD CLAIMS
THROUGH HER FATHER JAMES
THE MONARCHS AGREED TO GO DUTCH.

The rule of husband-and-wife team William and Mary was essentially an invasion dressed up as a revolution – they were installed as job-sharing co-monarchs on the basis that a vacancy existed as her dad James II had abdicated by doing a runner. Where it became revolutionary was in the rights parliament then gained through negotiation, limiting the monarch's power to raise taxes, declare war, etc.

They also slipped in a few clauses about the royal succession (basically, 'No Catholics, no spouses of Catholics'). They encountered some opposition from supporters of James in the Highlands and in Ireland, where English forces intervened in support of the Protestant minority.

When Mary died in 1694, William struggled on alone, but it wasn't the same – their friends were so used to them being an item they used to call them Williamnmary. They were the Brangelina of their day.

William III and Mary II

Ruled England, Wales, Scotland, Ireland, 1689–1702 (him); 1689–1694 (her).
Monarchs because Grandson of Charles I/daughter of James II – and
invasion. **First language** Dutch (him); English (her).

IS IT MY TURN TO BE KING NOW? MOST TENUOUS SUCCESSIONS

GEORGE I

JAMES I'S GREAT-GRANDSON

Fifty-first in line, *nichts Englisch sprechen*. Protestant? Come on over!

HENRY IV

GRANDSON OF EDWARD III

Only fifth in line when Richard II was forced to abdicate. But he made the succession his.

JANE GREY

KING HENRY VII'S GREAT-GRANDDAUGHTER

Third in line, her succession went against Henry VIII's Third Succession Act. It didn't wash.

WILLIAM AND MARY

Fourth and second in line respectively once they had chased James II away – and they didn't do that just to install his son James!

RICHARD III

EDWARD IV'S BROTHER

Actually next in succession, so not that tenuous. But the only obstacle, Edward's young son Edward, conveniently disappeared.

ANNE

THERE WAS AN OLD MONARCH CALLED ANNE
WHO WENT BY THE NAME BRANDY NAN.
UNHEALTHY AND STOUT,
AFFLICTED BY GOUT,
SHE RODE IN A SPECIAL SEDAN.

Queen Anne was the last of the Stuarts, which threatened to reopen the
question of whether Scotland should have its own king. To head this off,
England and Scotland were joined by the 1707 Act of Union, and Great
Britain was born.

  Poor Anne had five children who all died in childhood, as well as
a dozen more miscarriages or stillbirths. She also had a complicated set
of health problems, including gout, leaving her effectively lame from
her thirties onwards. Under the circumstances, her attachment to a
drop of the hard stuff is understandable, but may not have helped.

Anne

Ruled England, Wales, Scotland (called Great Britain from 1707), Ireland,
1702–1714. **Queen because** Her father James was king (and she wasn't
Catholic). **Age at accession** 37.   **Religion** Protestant.

GEORGE I

A GERMAN, GEORGE LUDWIG, FROM HANOVER
CAME IN, WITH THE REIGN OF QUEEN ANNE OVER.
SELECTION WAS HARD
WITH CATHOLICS BARRED,
SO PARLIAMENT SHIPPED THE OLD MAN OVER.

George I was chosen as Anne's successor over 50 other contenders because they were all Catholics. If he'd had to pass a language test, never mind a citizenship test, he'd have failed miserably. George didn't even like Britain much, preferring his native Hanover in Germany. And his wife didn't come to join him, though that was because he locked her in a tower for having an affair.

The new king's grasp of English was pretty much limited to ordering a beer, and even that went wrong because when he kept asking for 'A beer, bitte', when he actually wanted lager. A long-lasting consequence of this language barrier was the creation of the post of prime minister – initially required to run things while the king practised his English verbs. The first one was Robert Walpole, who was fortunately able to communicate with His Majesty in Latin.

George I

Ruled Great Britain and Ireland, 1714–1727. **King because** His great-grandad James I was (and he wasn't Catholic). **Position in succession (including Catholics)** 51st. **Languages** 1) German, 2) Latin, 3) French. Not English.

GEORGE II

THE SECOND KING GEORGE TOOK HIS CHANCE
TO HALT THE PRETENDER'S ADVANCE,
ENSURING OUR MONARCH
WAS ANGLO-TEUTONIC
INSTEAD OF A SCOTSMAN FROM FRANCE.

George II was also born in Germany — he was an adult by the time the Hanoverians became surprise winners of the royal lottery. His father had already had to resist a series of challenges from James II's 'warming-pan' son. Now the Old Pretender's son stepped up to the plate — Bonnie Prince Charlie, aka the Young Pretender.

The thing was, the Stuart family had by now spent so much time in France and Italy, they were a bit out of touch with politics in the UK, where the pro-Hanover Whigs were facing off against the Stuart-sympathising Tories. This meant Charlie was apt to believe the hype in the polls, wildly overestimating Tory support in Derby South and doing rash things like not waiting for the French army to join him before attacking. In 1746 he was finally defeated by the English army at Culloden. The royal family was to remain Anglo-German and Protestant, not Franco-Scottish and Catholic.

George II

Ruled Great Britain and Ireland, 1727–1760.
King because His dad George was. **First language** French/German.
Cause of death Heart attack while drinking cocoa on the toilet.

GEORGE III

THERE WAS AN OLD KING, GEORGE THE THIRD,
WHOSE ACTIONS WERE RATHER ABSURD.
AN UNKNOWN DISEASE
HAD HIM TALKING TO TREES,
HE WENT QUITE INSANE, IN A WORD.

George III was the first Hanoverian king to grow up in Britain, speaking English. Ironically, after the Treaty of Vienna in 1815 he was also the first to be King of Hanover itself, as well as Britain.

His 60-year reign saw massive changes – including the industrial revolution, the growth of the press and the colonisation of Australia and New Zealand. But George is mainly remembered for annoying the colonists of America so much with his tax rises and his intransigent attitude in the 1770s that they fought for and won independence.

Well, he's remembered for one other thing. George III suffered from episodes of madness that have been put down variously to porphyria, arsenic poisoning by his doctors and some kind of mental illness. On one occasion he is reported to have stopped to shake hands with a tree that he insisted was the King of Prussia. Friedrich Wych-elm, I presume!

George III

Ruled Great Britain and Ireland, 1760–1820 (UK from 1801); Hanover 1814–1820. **King because** His grandad George was.
First language English.   **Achievements** Losing America.

FRIEDRICH WILHELM I

FRED WILLIAM WAS QUITE ON THE BALL,
JUST ONE LITTLE WEAKNESS WAS ALL,
HE LIKED TO COLLECT,
THEN DRILL AND INSPECT
HIS GUARDS – AND THEY HAD TO BE TALL.

Friedrich Wilhelm I was a stern father – he wanted his son put to death for eloping with another man, but settled for just having the other man killed. But FW the elder had a thing about men himself – specifically tall ones. 'The most beautiful girl or woman in the world would be a matter of indifference to me, but tall soldiers – they are my weakness,' he said.

The king built up the guards corps nicknamed the Potsdam Giants by collecting tall soldiers (they had to be over six foot two, or 1.88m) from all over Europe – Irishman James Kirkland was seven feet tall. He even tried to persuade tall men to mate with tall women, to produce a new giant race.

Why did he go to such great lengths? Perhaps he just looked up to men of height – being about five foot two (1.6m) himself.

Friedrich Wilhelm I
Ruled Prussia, 1713–1740.
King because His dad Friedrich was.
Height Yes, please.

LUDWIG II

KING LUDWIG SPENT ALL THAT HE HAD
ON CASTLES, A PERSONAL FAD;
SO SHRINKS WERE ASSIGNED
TO GAUGE THE KING'S MIND,
PRONOUNCING HIM STARK RAVING MAD.

Just because you're paranoid, it doesn't mean they're not all out to get you – and in the case of Ludwig II of Bavaria they clearly were. A friend and admirer of the composer Richard Wagner, 'Mad King Ludwig' is fondly remembered these days as the eccentric behind the fairytale castle Neuschwanstein, which looks like a set from a Wagner opera.

But as king of a state that was subsumed by a united Germany in 1870, he had to answer to ministers for his spending, and they were not happy with his extravagant projects. So they appointed a panel of doctors to consider compelling evidence like 'he eats outdoors in all weathers' and declare him paranoid and mad. They came to take him away, but after a walk around the grounds of his castle with one of his doctors, both men were found dead in the shallow end of the lake.

Ludwig II

Ruled Bavaria, 1864–1886 (from 1870 part of Germany).
King because His dad Maximilian was.
Cause of death Mysterious.

GEORGE IV

A REGENT WHO WENT OFF THE RAILS
HIT SEVENTEEN STONE ON THE SCALES.
THE DRUG-TAKING GEORGIE
THOUGHT LIFE ONE BIG ORGY,
UNTIL HE BECAME PRINCE OF WHALES.

George III's imaginatively named son took the reins of power in 1811 as regent when the old man seriously lost his marbles, but was not crowned king until nine years later. At this point he unceremoniously ditched his wife Caroline, turning her away from the coronation and unsuccessfully trying to divorce her.

George was already a notorious party animal – a womaniser, flamboyant dresser, morbidly obese boozer and prodigious consumer of opium who racked up massive debts and ended up getting bailed out by the Treasury.

George ballooned, and was lampooned, cartooned and satirically harpooned – as the Prince of Whales.

George IV

Ruled United Kingdom of Great Britain and Ireland/Hanover, 1820–1830.
King because His dad George was.
Age at accession 57. **Waist** 50in (130cm).

WILLIAM IV

OLD BILL WAS A BIT OF A KNAVE,
ENJOYING A LIFE ON THE WAVE;
HAD WILLIAM'S OWN SEED
BEEN LEFT TO SUCCEED
WE MIGHT NOW BE RULED BY KING DAVE.

As a younger son, William didn't expect to be king, so he lived the normal life of a junior royal – travelling the world in the navy, getting arrested over a drunken brawl in Gibraltar, and hanging out with Lord Nelson. On George IV's death he became the oldest person to accede to the throne, aged 64.

As a young man, William was not allowed to marry without his brother's consent, so he cohabited with his mistress, the actress Dorothea Jordan, and had ten children with her. He later ditched her and made a proper royal match to try for heirs, but none survived.

William's niece Victoria succeeded him because his illegitimate offspring didn't count – if they had, we could have ended up with David Cameron as king!

William IV

Ruled United Kingdom of Great Britain and Ireland, 1830–1837.
King because His dad George was. **Nickname** Silly Billy. **Achievements** Last king to name a prime minister against parliament's wishes.

LEOPOLD II

WHEN BELGIAN KING LEO THE SECOND
GOT CONGO, PROSPERITY BECKONED,
HIS COFFERS WERE FILLED
WHILE MANY WERE KILLED,
TEN MILLION OR MORE, IT'S BEEN RECKONED.

Belgium was only created as an independent country in 1830, and Victoria's cousin King Leopold felt his new nation had missed out on the colonial spoils other Europeans had – 'a slice of this magnificent African cake', as he charmingly put it. He paid Henry Stanley to explore the Congo, securing control of an area 75 times the size of Belgium.

But Congo was not an official colony as such, it was Leopold's personal property, which the king exploited mercilessly, using forced labour to make his fortune from rubber. His mercenary army is estimated to have killed about half the population, committing atrocities such as cutting off the hands of those failing to meet their quotas.

Faced with mounting criticism, the grand theft autocrat's PR response was to ship hundreds of Congolese over to Brussels and put them on show in replica villages, like human zoos. He's not fondly remembered in Congo.

Leopold II

Ruled Belgium, 1865–1909.
King because His dad Leopold was.
Legacy Underdevelopment in central Africa.

VICTORIA

THERE WAS AN OLD QUEEN WITH A FROWN,
HER COUNTENANCE OFTEN CAST DOWN.
ONE MAN MADE HER FRISKY,
THE SCOT WITH THE WHISKY —
VICTORIA'S SECRET, JOHN BROWN.

Queen Victoria ruled for 63 years. Under her reign the British Empire expanded and great industries were created. But the Victorian era tends to be remembered for its prudery – which has been a bit exaggerated in the telling. There's little evidence for the popular story that Queen Victoria reacted to a risqué story from an equerry with the words 'We are not amused'. But the phrase seems to fit with the dour face that still looks down at us from hundreds of pub signs, so the story stuck.

Certainly she was deeply unhappy and withdrawn after the death of her much-loved German hubby Albert. The man credited with cheering her up was her Scottish manservant John Brown, who would put a tot of whisky in her tea. Her daughters called him 'Mama's lover', they slept in adjoining rooms, and some claim the couple were secretly married.

Victoria

Ruled United Kingdom of Great Britain and Ireland, 1837–1901; Empress of India, 1876–1901. **Queen because** Her grandad George III was king. **Legacy** Empire, railways, Irish famine, sexual repression.

EDWARD VII

THE TALES OF SAXE-COBURG AND GOTHA'LL LIVE ON IN LE CHABANAIS BROTHEL WHERE DIRTY OLD BERTIE, SO CHARMING AND FLIRTY, KEPT GOING LONG AFTER BETROTHAL.

Prince Albert of Saxe-Coburg and Gotha decided to use the name Edward on becoming king, tactfully saying he didn't want to diminish his late father's name. Yeah, right. Bertie, as he was known, reacted against his staid and prudish parents as a teenager by becoming a notorious libertine and pleasure-seeker. Sent for a spell with the army in Ireland, he enjoyed an illicit liaison with an actress. Two weeks later his father died, and Victoria blamed Bertie for shaming Albert to his grave.

Undeterred, Bertie carried on with numerous mistresses before and after engagement and marriage to Princess Alexandra of Denmark. And just to add a bit of spice, the Prince of Wales was a regular visitor to Le Chabanais brothel in Paris, whose delights included a champagne bath and a special Love Chair with numerous possible multi-player options.

Of course, all that stopped when he became king. Perhaps.

Edward VII

Ruled United Kingdom of Great Britain and Ireland and the British Dominions, 1901–1910. **King because** His mum Victoria was queen. **Nephews** Kaiser Wilhelm II of Germany; Tsar Nicholas II of Russia (by marriage).

GEORGE
V

AS EUROPE ERUPTED IN FLAMES
KING GEORGE FOUND HIS FAMILY NAMES
TOO CLOSE TO HIS FOES',
SO CHANGED THEM AND CHOSE
THE NAME OF A TOWN ON THE THAMES.

George V presided over a great deal of change – the primacy of elected politicians, universal suffrage, Labour's rise to government, the partition of Ireland and the deaths of millions of people as Europe was torn apart by the First World War.

At the beginning of the 20th century, most European countries were ruled by George's cousins. By the time the war ended in 1918, many of them had been swept aside, including Tsar Nicholas II of Russia, deposed and killed in the 1917 revolutions, and of course Kaiser Wilhelm II of Germany.

In the middle of the war, George finally decided the embarrassment of his German family links was too much. He changed the family name to Windsor, after Windsor Castle – disappointing writers of rude limericks, who were hoping he'd pick Buckingham Palace.

George V
Ruled United Kingdom of Great Britain and Ireland and the British Dominions, 1910–1936. **King because** His dad Edward was. **Distinguishing features** Manicured beard.

KAISER WILHELM II

THERE WAS AN OLD MAN FROM BERLIN
WHO FOUGHT WITH HIS BRITISHER KIN,
IT MIGHT HAVE BEEN WISER
IF WILHELM THE KAISER
HAD NOT LET THE GREAT WAR BEGIN.

Wilhelm was Queen Victoria's grandson and George V's cousin – there are pictures of him as a child dressed in a kilt. But though Victoria doted on him, and he looked up to her, the rest of the UK side of the family couldn't stand him.

His military build-up at the start of the 20th century bears some responsibility for Europe's drift into the First World War, and once it started and Britain needed a bogeyman, 'Kaiser Bill' fitted the bill perfectly.

After defeat in 1918 he was allowed to retire to the Netherlands, where he spent much of the next two decades bombarding Adolf Hitler with helpful advice (like 'why not restore the monarchy?') and ranting about how Britain had been taken over by Jews. Oddly, Churchill offered Britain's former enemy sanctuary when the Nazis invaded Holland in 1940, but he preferred to take his chances with Hitler.

Kaiser Wilhelm II

Ruled Germany, 1888–1918.
Kaiser because His dad Friedrich was.
Age at accession 29. **Died** 1941.

EDWARD VIII

OF KINGS, ED WAS ONE OF THE FLASHEST,
HIS LOVE LIFE WAS SURELY THE RASHEST;
HIS SWIFT ABDICATION
AT LEAST SPARED THE NATION
A KING WHO WAS RATHER A FASCIST.

'After I am dead,' George V declared of his playboy son Edward, 'the boy will ruin himself within a year.' Harsh but fair – Edward VIII ruled for just under 11 months before being forced to abdicate over his determination to marry the American divorcee Wallis Simpson. At the time this was a great scandal. Apart from anything else, the king was head of the Church of England, which did not approve of such marriages.

Nowadays his reputation is more harmed by other things – like his comparing native Australians to monkeys, or being rude and racist about the black inhabitants of the Bahamas when he was governor there. And there's the small matter of his friendship with Adolf Hitler. It is widely believed that, had the Nazis conquered Britain, Hitler would have put Edward back on the throne.

Edward VIII

Ruled United Kingdom of Great Britain and Ireland and the British Dominions, 20 January–11 December 1936.
King because His dad George was. **Age at accession** 41.

GEORGE VI

OLD BERTIE, THE KING OF THE BRITS,
STAYED PUT THROUGH THE YEARS OF THE BLITZ,
WITH BOMBS RAINING DOWN
ON OLD LONDON TOWN —
HIS PAD TOOK A COUPLE OF HITS.

George VI was another Bertie but, like his grandfather Edward VII, he spurned the name Albert, choosing to rule under his third middle name, George. Which must have been a bit odd for his youngest brother – George!

The new king was a lot less flamboyant than his Nazi-loving brother Ed, and struggled with a stammer, which made the public speaking side of his job an issue – eventually resolved with the help of a speech therapist.

In a break from tradition, George married a woman he quite liked, Elizabeth Bowes-Lyon, who was not even royal – her dad was only an earl! But the two of them improved the image of the royal family no end by staying in London throughout the bombing campaigns of the Second World War, even though two bombs fell on Buckingham Palace. Admittedly, they did usually go back to their castle at Windsor to sleep.

George VI

Ruled United Kingdom of Great Britain and Ireland and the British Dominions, 1936–1952.
King because His dad George was.   **Age at accession** 41.

ELIZABETH II

THERE WAS AN OLD WOMAN NAMED LIZ
WHO WORKED IN THE ROYALTY BIZ,
WITH YEARS ON THE THRONE
TO MAKE IT HER OWN,
WHILE CHARLES WAITED TILL IT WAS HIS.

Little did those singing the national anthem after Queen Elizabeth II's coronation back in 1953 know how accurate the line 'long to reign over us' was to prove. In September 2015 she surpassed Queen Victoria's record of 63 years, 216 days on the throne. And that period, like Victoria's, has been one of massive transformation – the independence of former British colonies, space travel, corgi videos on YouTube... and, of course, the monarchy had to change with it in order to survive. Royal announcements are now made on Twitter and, in her Diamond Jubilee year, the Queen even played along with a film pretending she had parachuted into the 2012 London Olympic Games.

The law of succession was altered in 2013 to remove the disqualification of anyone who happened to have married a Catholic – and to allow sons and daughters equal treatment in the royal line-up. Not that this will make any difference for ages – Prince Charles is still heir to the throne, as he has been since the age of three.

Elizabeth II

Ruled United Kingdom of Great Britain and Northern Ireland; Head of Commonwealth, 1952–present. **Queen because** Her dad George was king. **Age at accession** 25. **Achievements** Longest reign.

COMPOSING MY LIMERICK VERSE
I'VE OFT HAD OCCASION TO CURSE
THE CHOICE OF THE SAME
UNRHYMABLE NAME
LIKE WILLIAM, OR HENRY, OR WORSE.

OK, I admit, the limerick part would have been easier if the royals hadn't insisted on using the same names over and over. Especially ones like 'Henry' that don't rhyme with anything. Not to mention the shifting selection of ordinal numbers between 'first' and 'eighth', most of which also pose a stiff rhyming challenge.

And it's not getting any better – the succession list after Elizabeth goes Charles, William, George, Charlotte, Henry...! Come on, folks, let's have a Joe or Jo, or a Ray. Or maybe it's time for King Mick.

THE AUTHOR, AS EVER, DEPENDS
ON EDITOR, FAMILY AND FRIENDS,
BUT SHOULD RHYME OR WITTICISM
COME IN FOR CRITICISM,
MINE IS THE HAND THAT OFFENDS.

Thanks are due once more to my family of historians and history-lovers, especially to Anna, Gerry, Rosa and Eva, who all improved my efforts with ideas and amendments. Also of course to Katie and Nicola at Pavilion, for all their hard work in ensuring the old geezer called Caesar had a royal successor.

And I take this opportunity to thank all those who have followed, retweeted, liked, shared and otherwise interacted with my daily news limericks at twitter.com/twitmericks, at facebook.com/twitmericks, and at twitmericks.com.

Illustrations by Hannah Warren / JellyLondon.com

ALSO BY MICK TWISTER

THERE WAS AN OLD GEEZER CALLED CAESAR: A HISTORY OF THE WORLD IN 100 LIMERICKS

First published in the United Kingdom in 2017 by
Portico
1 Gower Street
London
WC1E 6HD

An imprint of Pavilion Books Company Ltd

ISBN 978-1-91104-223-5

A CIP catalogue record for this book is available from the British Library.

10 9 8 7 6 5 4 3 2 1

Reproduction by Mission Productions Ltd, Hong Kong
Printed and bound by 1010 Printing International Ltd, China

This book can be ordered direct from the publisher at www.pavilionbooks.com